The

Joyful Mysteries

of Life

Catherine and Bernard Scherrer

FAMILY PUBLICATIONS

•

IGNATIUS PRESS

Originally published under the title
Les mystères joyeux de la vie

Cover design by Joanna Pitt

published by
Family Publications
77 Banbury Road, Oxford, UK
ISBN 1-871217-19-9

Ignatius Press
San Francisco, USA
ISBN 0-89870-630-0

Printed in England

Contents

Editor's Note

This book was first published in French in 1994 under the title *Les mystères joyeux de la vie*. It has already proved so popular that editions in Spanish, German, Hungarian and Polish are now in preparation. This English translation is by Patricia Hardcastle, and I am also indebted to Léonie and Stratford Caldecott, Fr Richard Duffield and others for their help with editing.

The book was written for parents and their children. The words 'mother' and 'father' have been used to translate *Maman* and *Papa* but parents should feel free to substitute alternative English words as appropriate to their own family situation. Similarly, for the sake of brevity, a baby is referred to as 'he' rather than 'he or she'.

I am grateful to His Eminence Cardinal López Trujillo for his encouragement and for his foreword. It is hoped that the book will be helpful to parents and children in this sensitive area, and that it will supplement the important document *The Truth and Meaning of Human Sexuality: Guidelines for Education within the Family* recently published by the Pontifical Council for the Family.

Denis Riches

Foreword

The publication of *The Truth and Meaning of Human Sexuality: Guidelines for Education within the Family* (Pontifical Council for the Family, 1995) marked a new era in what is inadequately described as 'sex education', but which Pope John Paul II proposes as 'education for chastity' to be provided normally in the home (*Familiaris Consortio*, no. 37).

Nevertheless, the question remains: how are parents to carry out this right and duty in the home? This explains the call for good resources in *The Truth and Meaning of Human Sexuality*, no. 147.

I welcome the publication of an English translation of *Les Mystères Joyeux de la Vie* as a response to that call. With its predominantly spiritual and moral emphasis, in a positive, clear and delicate way, this book is designed to assist parents in their task of formation.

The important question 'when?' means that the decision concerning the timing of this education rests with the parents themselves (cf. *The Truth and Meaning of Human Sexuality*, nos. 65-67, 75-76 etc.). Each child is an individual person, developing at a different pace, therefore the authors rightly indicate that this book is not an inflexible programme.

The authors believe that parents are *the* people to give an education in the mysteries of the beginning of life. In practice, other agencies can and do help parents, but the role of others is always to be *subordinate* and *subsidiary*, nor are parents bound to accept help if they believe they can fulfil this task themselves (cf. *The Truth and Meaning of Human*

Sexuality, nos. 145-146). They must also discern the method and content of assistance that others provide. But those who use this book should also find that it helps them to judge the quality of assistance, when it is being offered.

May all the parents who take up this book be guided in their task by the intercession of the ever-virgin Mother of God, who reigns as the Queen of the Family.

Alfonso Cardinal López Trujillo
*President of the Pontifical Council
for the Family*

Introduction

Dear Parents,

This book was originally written with the aim of providing our own children with a Christian presentation of the facts of life. Friends encouraged us to publish it to help other parents who find their children asking questions about sex well before their teenage years.

It is natural for parents to be unsure about the ideal age to present information on this subject. In the past, it was possible to wait longer because a good school and decent social environment allowed children to keep their innocence at least until puberty. But in today's world parents should talk clearly and frankly to their children in responding to their questions, for if they do not, it may be too late. Others may step in to supply the information in undesirable and damaging ways.

In tackling sexual matters with their children parents have to steer a course between two extremes. On the one hand there is a materialism which typically involves both a harmful clinical coldness and a mindless hedonism. This approach brings the love of husband and wife, and the gift of a new life created in the image and likeness of God, down to a base or commonplace level. On the other hand, there is a puritanism which treats everything to do with the body as bad or dirty. This attitude affects us more deeply than we realise. Who has not said to a little child, very naturally discovering those organs which the good Lord has given him: 'Don't touch, that's dirty!' But how can anything be dirty which has an important role in the genesis of new life? However delicate a matter it is to talk about, we should never forget that our procreative power is amongst the most respectable and indeed astonishing things.

Bearing in mind these concerns, we have used two guides to find the right tone in writing about this subject: wonder and chastity. The procreative 'mechanism' (for want of a better term) is amongst the greatest mysteries of creation – not only the development of a new person from the very moment of conception, but also the preparation of our bodies for that moment, meticulously planned in the wisdom and prudence of God. Our bodies are ordered to fertility, and only take on their full meaning in the light of this purpose.

Chastity, then, does not mean detaching ourselves from the procreative side of our nature, but rather living it out as God wills, according to our state in life, following the order of divine love, and enlightened as much by prudence as by charity. The teachings of the Church on the way to do this, particularly those of the Popes, have not changed, and (setting aside questions of style) it is very difficult to tell whether a particular instruction or encyclical has come from Pius XII, Paul VI or John Paul II.

We believe that parents are *the* people who should give children their education in the mysteries of the beginning of life! The whole subject is so important that it should not be delegated to schools or other agencies. The family, not the school, is at the heart of the mystery we are considering – though the school and others should assist parents with good moral catechesis.

This little book, placed under the protection of the Holy Family, is intended to foster vocations not only to marriage but also to the priesthood and religious life. After all, the life of consecrated virginity only has meaning in a social context of flourishing family life. The Church needs both foundations for its ascent to God, and experience shows that they tend to decline or flourish together.

The best approach to this book is to regard it simply as a tool to be used, not as an inflexible programme. Some parents will want to tell their children everything at once, at the age they deem appropriate, while others will attempt a more gradual introduction, taking into account the questions asked by their children, and the opportunities thrown up by day-to-day life.

But certainly children must nowadays be well informed before they reach secondary school, where many and various abominations are waiting, not least the official sex education programmes, and worse still the peer-group attitudes of cunning and mockery. Above all young girls need to have been fully informed by their parents in advance of their first periods. Fertility is the key to the understanding they need to have.

Parents must not mince their words. Boys have the right to know that girls are 'tabernacles' of the mystery of life, and that they must be respected as such. They should know that this tabernacle has been sealed by God, and that he who breaks the seal without the right to do so is committing a profanity if he knows what he is doing, or else an act of mindless irresponsibility. Girls must know that boys are more liable to temptation, and that it is not good to add to their burden by a lack of modesty, or by ambivalent attitudes or behaviour.

Parents should of course live up to their own teaching if the education they give is to bear fruit. To take one example: parents who use contraception cannot honestly ask their children not to use it. Children have a special, almost supernatural gift for reading their parents' hearts and the secrets which are kept there, so deception is never successful.

They may not find out the physical details, which are not really important in any case, but they detect the principles at work. If parents' primary concern is for their own personal fulfilment, this will determine the message about marriage conveyed to their children (unless grace intervenes). If their primary concern is for the mystical significance of their marriage, God's gift of each to the other, in other words for charity, then this message will come across just as strongly. Of course God will (through the sacraments) give parents all the graces they need for their own conversion of heart. The purpose of family life is identical with that of life itself: to make us into saints, for our own salvation and that of our neighbours, through Christ, with Christ and in Christ.

Of course this struggle for sanctity within the home must go hand-in-hand with the battle which is currently being fought out in the public arena over abortion, the misuse of foetuses, and the cheapening of youthful sexual relations under cover of the fight against AIDS. This is surely the very conflict described in chapter twelve of the Apocalypse of St John. It is another battle which we have already lost if we count only on our own resources, but in which victory is sure if we depend entirely on Christ.

Finally, for the sake of parents who may still be anxious about depriving their children of their innocence at an early age, perhaps we should take a look, with God, at Adam and Eve before the Fall. God saw that it was *very good*, when in the full light of day 'they were both naked, and were not ashamed' (*Gen* 2:25). St Paul tells us that we are children of the light, and the light is what Satan fears most of all.

Let us take St Anne for our model in education. Her daughter at the age of fifteen could answer the angel Gabriel at the Annunciation perfectly frankly and directly:

'How shall this be, seeing I know not a man' (*Lk* 1:34).

Our Lady's answer manifests the light, the light of the children of God.

May she help us and keep us, and our children.

Catherine and Bernard Scherrer

1

The cradle of the tiniest babies

Can you remember a baby being born? Perhaps you can remember the birth of a little brother or sister, or a cousin, or a new baby for friends or relatives.

I'm sure you will have noticed that just before the baby is born, his mother prepares a cradle for him. She puts pretty sheets in it, and cosy blankets or a soft little duvet, and she might put in a holy medal tied with a ribbon as well. All of this is done very carefully and lovingly by parents for the baby they are expecting, although they don't know him yet.

Have you ever wondered what the baby's cradle was before he was born, and who prepared it? Before he is born, the baby's cradle is in his mother's tummy, and it is called the *womb* (doctors call it the *uterus*). It is a very soft little cradle which God, our creator, who especially loves little babies, gives to each girl, so that if, one day, she becomes a mother, she can cradle her baby for the nine months of his life before he is born.

The womb is in the tummy of little girls, young women and mums, below the tummy button. It is the same size and shape as an avocado pear. The Japanese call it 'shy kyu' which means 'Palace of the Child'. It is certainly very comfortable for the little baby who settles down there at the beginning of his life. At that point the baby is the size of a pin-head, and doesn't really look like a baby at all. Sometimes his parents aren't at first aware that he exists, but God realises, because he has already given him a soul and loved him.

Once he is settled in his mother's womb, the baby grows. Three weeks after the beginning of his life, his heart starts to beat. When he is ten weeks, he has little hands and feet, and his tiny face is taking shape. By the time he is twelve weeks he is already trying to suck his thumb! By four or five months, his mother can feel him moving. Her womb grows with the baby and her tummy gets rounder as the baby starts to take up space. His hidden life goes on for nine months.

Do you know about the *Visitation*? If you know how to pray the *Rosary*, something which greatly pleases Our Lady, our mother in heaven, then you will know that it is the second Joyful Mystery of the Rosary. The Visitation was the visit of Mary to her cousin Elizabeth. Mary was carrying Jesus inside her. Because Jesus was very tiny, only a few days old, no one could see or know that she was *pregnant* (the word we use when a woman is carrying a child inside her). Elizabeth was also pregnant. The child in her womb was St John the Baptist, who was six months older than Jesus.

Mary went to help her cousin Elizabeth, who was quite old and tired by her *pregnancy*, until John was born. When Elizabeth opened the door to Mary, the baby John sensed the presence of Jesus (God the Son, the Messiah) and leapt for joy. Elizabeth was filled with the Holy Spirit and realised in her turn that Mary was carrying the Saviour of the world. She said to Mary 'Blessed art thou amongst women and blessed is the fruit of thy womb Jesus'. These words have been made part of the *Hail Mary*, a prayer I'm sure you will know already. (If you don't remember it, ask your mother or father to teach it to you again.)

A doctor would have said 'of your uterus', which would have been more precise, if less poetic. Certainly the uterus, or womb, is a very cosy cradle, and Jesus spent some of his most pleasant time on earth there.

Questions

What do we call a baby's cradle before he is born?
What does a doctor call it?

How long is it from the moment God gives a baby life until he is born?

Does he look like a little baby when God gives him life?

How old is he when his heart starts to beat? Have you ever seen photos of a baby in the first weeks of his life?

Who was St Elizabeth?

What do we call the second mystery of the Rosary?
Would you like to say it now?

Have you read the story of the Visitation in St Luke's Gospel (chapter 1, verses 39-56)? Why not ask someone to help you find it.

What are the words of St Elizabeth that we say in the *Hail Mary?*

How did St Elizabeth know that Our Lady was carrying the Saviour of the World?

Do you say the Hail Mary regularly? When? Why? What about trying to say it every day, out of love for Jesus and Mary? You could try when you first get up, or before you go to bed, or even both!

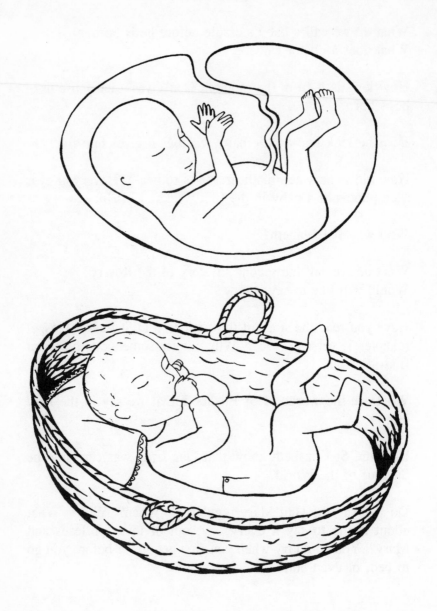

2

God prepares a cradle
for a tiny baby in every woman

Do you know how a baby gets food when he is inside his mother? And do you know why you have a tummy button?

The tummy button (which doctors call the *navel*) is the mark left by the *umbilical cord*. The umbilical cord joins the baby to his mother while he is in her uterus. The baby uses it to get food: his blood goes through the umbilical cord to the *placenta*. The placenta is an organ which the baby makes to help him get food from his mother's blood. So to feed her baby, his mother needs more blood than usual.

But what happens when a mother isn't expecting a baby? Each month, every woman's uterus prepares itself to receive a baby. The wall of the uterus covers itself with a lining (like a kind of quilt or duvet) which is very soft and very rich in blood, so that if a new baby settles there, it finds a comfortable cradle where it won't be disturbed. If no baby settles there, the lining leaves the woman's body through a kind of bleeding. This bleeding is known as *menstruation* or *a period*.

How can the period come out of the uterus? God has given girls and women a passage which joins the uterus to the outside. It is very delicate and clean and is called the *vagina*. It comes out in a place which is hidden behind the place where urine comes out. It is important not to confuse these two different places.

So this is how girls, when they are old enough, and mothers, when they are not expecting a baby, have a period about once a month (sometimes a bit less often) and lose the blood lining the uterus. In some countries, when a girl has her first period, it is a big family occasion. In any case, it is always a moment of great joy for parents to know that their daughter is growing up and one day may be a mother herself.

For the girl it marks her entry into the grown-up world in which everyone is responsible for what they do. When God endows a girl with *the gift of fertility* (fertility is being able to have children), he shows that he has a lot of trust in her. In a way he gives her some of his power to create new life. She must try to be worthy of this trust, even if God gives it automatically and without asking for anything in return. This gift is very special, but it can be damaged because of infection or disease, so it must be treasured. Just as your body is the temple of the Holy Spirit, so too you must guard God's gift of fertility and not spoil it or abuse it.

Mary was fifteen when the angel Gabriel came to ask her if she would be the mother of Jesus. This occasion we call the *Annunciation*, the first of the joyful mysteries of the Rosary. Mary may have had her first period some time earlier.

She was very good, very pure and very kind. She had never ceased to love God, and had given herself completely to him. She prayed hard and was always ready to help everybody around her. She had never sinned. She took great care of her body and had already consecrated herself to God without knowing what he was going to ask her to do.

What a big responsibility Mary was given at the Annunciation! If she had not been so good and kind, if there had been even the tiniest bit of selfishness or vanity in her heart, she would surely have refused to be the mother of Jesus, and we might not have been saved from Original Sin.

14

Questions

What does the umbilical cord do? And what about the placenta?

How does God prepare a woman's uterus for the baby she might one day have?

What is the lining of the womb mostly made of?

What happens if there is no baby to settle in it?

What do we call the flow of blood that comes from a woman about once a month?

Where does it come out of the woman's body?
Does the urine come the same way?

What does fertility mean?

Why is it such a great responsibility?

What happened at the Annunciation?

3

The baby is born

For nine months, the baby grows inside his mother. It is amazing how quickly he grows. At the start of his life he is the size of a pin-head; nine months later he weighs about 7 lbs (or sometimes a little more) and is about 20 inches long. While he is in his mother's womb, he normally points his head downwards and his arms and legs are curled up to occupy as little room as possible. But his mother's tummy is nevertheless very big and round by the time he is born. By then his head is about 4 inches in diameter. Do you or your sister have a doll which is about the size of a baby just before he is born?

How can the baby come out of his mother? God decided he should come through the vagina, the same way as a period. But how can a baby of such size pass through a channel which seems to be so small?

Well, as you know the womb is very small when there is no baby inside it, but grows as the baby inside it grows. The vagina also changes in the last days of pregnancy, and grows wider at the moment of birth to let the baby come through.

A few hours before the birth, his mother starts to feel *contractions*. This is how she knows that her baby is ready to be born. Her husband takes her to the *maternity unit* (the special part of a hospital where birth takes place). The baby is born after some hours and takes his first breath.

The birth of the baby is usually very tiring for his mother, as it requires great effort, and is sometimes quite painful as well. So she stays in bed for a few days to recover, before

17

returning home to look after all her children. But of course these first few days are a great joy for the parents, because they give them their first opportunity get to know the most recent addition to their family, whom they have loved for nine months already.

When do we celebrate the birth of Jesus? At Christmas, of course! In France Christmas is called *Noël*, a word from old French which means 'a cry of joy'.

Do you remember what happened to Mary and Joseph on Christmas Eve? There was no room for them at the inns in Bethlehem, and so they were forced to stay in a cave used as a stable. You know about the ox and the ass which kept the baby Jesus warm as he lay in the manger, and the shepherds, awakened by the angels, who came to *adore* him.

'To adore' means 'to recognise that someone is God' – even if today some people use the word when they just mean that they love something or someone a lot. The shepherds really could *adore* Jesus, because Jesus is God the Son, but if you say that you adore ice cream, or your little brother, it doesn't mean the same thing at all!

Jesus was born from Mary like sunlight passing through a fine crystal. The birth did not change her body at all. That is why at evening prayer in the days after Christmas, after the anthem to Our Lady, this short prayer is said:

> O Virgin, when you became a mother, your body preserved its integrity. Mother of God, pray for us.

The *Nativity* (the birth of Jesus) is the third Joyful Mystery of the Rosary. We have already looked at the first, the *Annunciation*, and the second, the *Visitation*.

Do you know about the last two Mysteries, *The Presentation of Jesus in the Temple*, and *The Finding of Jesus in the Temple*? If you don't, ask your parents, your grandparents or a priest to explain them to you, as they are also very beautiful. Then you will be able to pray all five Joyful Mysteries of the Rosary. You could also learn the five Sorrowful Mysteries and the five Glorious Mysteries. Our Lady loves it when we recall these moments in her life while praying the Rosary with her for the world.

Questions

How big is the baby when he is born?

How does a mother know her baby is ready to be born?

How does he come out of his mother?

Why does she rest after the birth of her baby?

What do parents feel when the baby is born? And what do the brothers and sisters feel?

What is the third Joyful Mystery of the Rosary?

What are the first three mysteries?

What are the last two mysteries called?

What are the other two sets of mysteries? Can you name them? And tell me what they are about?

Do you know how to pray the Rosary? Do you have a rosary?

Have you ever heard monks or nuns singing the Divine Office? Have you been to a monastery?

4

The vocations of women

If parents love one another, then they want their love to bring forth new life.

If the mother has good health, and if God permits, they will have a large family, because children are always a gift from God. St Catherine of Siena, who was a great saint and saved the Church when it was in great danger, was the 24th child in her family!

They will have a smaller family if the mother's age or health makes a large one impossible. Sometimes married couples just can't have children, however much they would like to.

You might think that God does something pointless when every month he prepares in every girl and mother a little cradle for a baby who in most cases doesn't arrive. It's also the case that unmarried as well as married women have a period every month for a good part of their lives (until they are about 45) – even nuns, who have consecrated themselves entirely to Jesus.

But then, even the death of Jesus on the Cross could seem to us to be pointless, although that is how we have all been saved from sin and death. And it is by cheerfully offering all the little sufferings and worries of our life on earth to Jesus (and periods are only a small part of this), as well as all our efforts to do good, that we can help Jesus to save souls.

St Paul wrote:

> In my flesh I complete what is lacking in Christ's afflictions (*Col* 1:24)

This doesn't mean that something is missing from Jesus' sufferings, which were the most terrible a man could undergo. It simply means that when we offer our lives to Jesus, he uses our offering to save the whole world.

If a young woman, or a religious, or a mother who is unable to have more children, offers to Jesus the pain her periods cause, and offers along with it any other sorrows she may have, he will unite her sufferings with his for the salvation of souls.

God has specially arranged that the hearts and bodies of women should be capable of loving as Jesus did, and also of sharing a little of Jesus' sufferings. When they offer to Jesus everything that love enables them to do, along with all their joys and sorrows, they can do a great deal of good in this world, for their families, for all the people they come across, and for the whole Church. They can also do a lot of good for the holy souls in Purgatory who need all the help we can give them.

All of this is called *spiritual fertility*. The vocation of a girl is really to fertility – both bodily and spiritual.

This spiritual fertility is how a nun, who offers her whole life to Jesus, can be as much of a 'mother' as a woman who has a family of twelve children. The nun's children are all those for whom she prays and offers herself every day.

St Thérèse of the Child Jesus was a Carmelite nun, who left Lisieux in France only once, in order to visit the Holy Father in Rome. During her life on earth she prayed especially for missionary priests and nuns, and after she died she was given the title of Patroness of Missions by the Church. So now she is the mother of all the missionaries for whom she prayed, and looks after them from heaven. When she was dying she said that she would spend eternity in heaven doing good on earth.

Remember also Mary, the Blessed Virgin. She had only one child on earth, Jesus, God the Son. But she was so closely united with her son, and offered herself so completely to God, keeping nothing for herself, that Jesus gave her to us as our Mother. She is the heavenly Mother of everyone on earth – and so by far the most fertile mother of all.

Questions

What do you know about the lives of St Catherine of Siena and St Thérèse of Lisieux? Ask somebody to tell you about them, or to lend you books about them.

Even if their periods seem to be pointless, how can a girl, or a nun, or a mother who can't have children, put them to good use?

What does Jesus do with our joys and our sorrows when we offer them to him?

Can a nun, who doesn't have children in a bodily way, be fertile?

What is this fertility called?

Do you offer your life to Jesus every day? Why?

Why do the holy souls in Purgatory need our prayers?

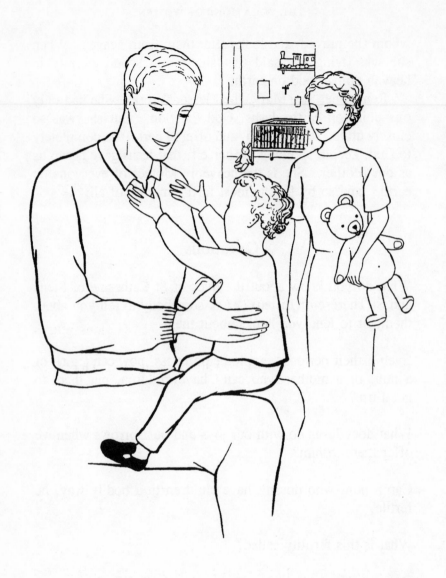

5

The role of the father

So far we haven't said much about the role of the father in giving life to little babies. He must play an important role, or no one would ever say that you or your brothers or sisters looked like him.

Out of pure love God created human beings to be male and female so that they could marry, and so that, being creative in his image, they could give life to children out of love.

Also, he doesn't want the mother to have to look after a baby all by herself – you can see that! It would mean that the baby had no father to love and protect him. God, who loves children so much, wouldn't want that!

So, while he prepares a cradle for the baby in each woman (the womb or uterus), he also gives her a special cell to go towards making a new baby. This special cell is called the *ovum*, which is the Latin word for an egg.

Every month one ovum is released by one of the two small organs called *ovaries* which each woman has. She has two in case one doesn't work. When they are both working they take it in turns to produce the egg.

The moment when one of the ovaries produces an egg is called *ovulation*. It takes place about two weeks before the start of a period.

This ovum or cell cannot make a new life on its own. If the mother is to have a baby, she needs the father to give her another cell. If he doesn't do this, the ovum very quickly dies and is lost with the period.

As you know, the bodies of men are different from those of women, and the special cells that fathers produce to make new life are very different from those produced by mothers. A man's cells are called *sperm* and are made by glands called *testicles*.

The father in fact gives a large number of sperm to the mother (about 250 million at a time!), and it is God who decides which of the father's cells he will unite to the mother's egg to make a new baby.

The instant when God makes new life by joining these two cells is called *conception*. The new baby doesn't yet have legs, arms, a mouth or eyes, but he or she is already a complete new human being, conceived in the image and likeness of God, and destined by God to live for eternity.

You are unique, then, because God lovingly chose the particular cell from your mother and the particular cell from your father (from 250 million possibilities!) which came together when your life began. It is because you are unique that God loves you and knows you by your name. He knew you as soon as he had created you, and he loved you even before your parents knew that you existed!

Read Psalm 138 (ask your parents to help you to find it). It is a wonderful prayer to God:

> For thou didst form my inward parts,
> thou didst knit me together in my mother's womb.
> My frame was not hidden from thee,
> when I was being made in secret . . .
> Thy eyes beheld my unformed substance.
> (verses 13, 15, 16).

You must be wondering what the father does to give his cells to the mother in order to create a new life.

He puts them into her vagina, the precious passage through which the baby will be born. So it is through the same channel that the mother both receives and in turn gives new life. Using his penis the father sends his sperm through the mother's vagina in a very beautiful gesture of love which expresses the union of their hearts, their souls and their bodies. The way this happens is a special secret between your parents, which they are telling you about because they love you and have confidence in you. But it is a very private matter which you shouldn't talk about with other people, but keep to yourself. It goes to the heart of the love between your parents, and if you talk about it you may spoil it and make them suffer. If you want to talk about it, talk about it only with your parents, or others you are sure you can trust.

If you marry when you are grown up, you will be able to share this with the person you marry. You should keep it in your heart and entrust it in your turn to your children when the time is right. By doing this you will be doing just what Our Lady did with the secrets God gave her: she kept them lovingly in her heart.

Let's talk a little more about Mary. You know when it was that Jesus began his life on earth: it was at the moment of the *Annunciation*. Jesus didn't have a father on earth to bring about his conception. He didn't need one, because his father is God the Father. What is more, Jesus is God the Son, and so he existed in heaven even before the world was created. But of course he did need a foster-father on earth to protect him while he was a child, and this foster-father was St Joseph.

God the Father performed a miracle so that his Son Jesus could become a tiny baby inside Mary's womb without any earthly father being involved. He did this by sending the Holy Spirit to Mary. We say that '*Mary conceived of the Holy Spirit*', whereas an ordinary baby is conceived by his parents. This great and beautiful mystery is called the *Incarnation*, and we remember it when we say the *Angelus*.

27

The Angelus is a very beautiful prayer that is said three times a day, at about seven in the morning, at midday, and at about six in the evening. ('Angelus' is the Latin word for angel, and 'angel' comes from a Greek word meaning 'messenger').

The Angel of the Lord declared unto Mary
And she conceived of the Holy Spirit
Hail Mary . . . .

Behold the handmaid of the Lord
Be it done to me according to thy word
Hail Mary . . . .

And the word was made flesh
And dwelt among us
Hail Mary . . . .

Pray for us, O Holy Mother of God.
That we may be made worthy of the promises of Christ

Let us pray.

Pour forth we beseech thee O Lord thy grace into our hearts that we to whom the Incarnation of Christ thy Son was made known by the message of an angel, may by his passion and cross, be brought to the glory of his resurrection. Through the same Christ our Lord. *Amen.*

Questions

What is the name of the special cell which comes from your mother and helps create a new baby? Does it have a soul?

28

What is the special cell from your father called?
Does it have a soul?

When God unites these two cells, one from your mother and one from your father, does the tiny baby have legs straightaway? Or arms? Or a mouth?

Does the baby have a soul straightaway?

How long does the baby's soul live? And what about yours?

What do we call the moment when God unites the two cells?

How do you know that you are unique, and that God wanted you to be exactly the person you are?

Why is it necessary not to talk about the beautiful privacy of your parents' love?

Can you name the three persons of the Holy Trinity? Are we talking about three gods? (If you aren't sure how to answer this question, ask your parents or a priest to explain the mystery of the Holy Trinity as soon as you can.)

What did the angel say to Mary at the Annunciation? What did Mary reply to the angel? (If you aren't sure read St Luke's Gospel, chapter 1, verses 26-38, with your mother or father).

What mystery took place at the Annunciation? What is it called?

Who is Jesus' father? Who is St Joseph?

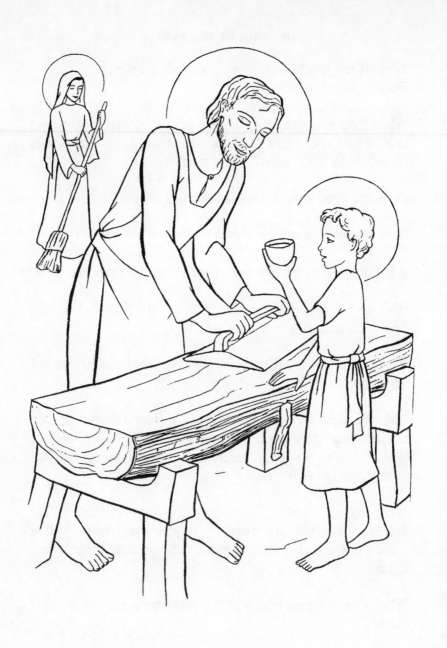

6

The vocations of men

We have spoken about the vocations of young women, and it is now time to talk about the vocations of young men.

Most young men are, of course, intended to be fathers. The young man who gets married has to love his wife and children, protect them, and work to provide a home, food and clothes for them. These are called the *duties of a father's state of life*.

The *duties of our state of life* are what God expects us to do in the circumstances in which we find ourselves. The duties of a schoolboy are to love God, to pray, to love his parents and brothers and sisters, to obey his parents, to work hard at school and respect his teachers, and to be kind and friendly to his classmates.

We have already described the duties of a father: to love God and to pray to him, to love his wife and children, to take the time to look after his children's education, and to work in order to give them a roof over their heads, sufficient food and everything they need for body and soul.

St Joseph, Jesus' foster-father, had a very important duty: to be the protector of Jesus and Mary. This wasn't always easy. When Jesus was a tiny baby, for example, St Joseph had to take his family on a donkey to Egypt to flee from Herod's anger.

Joseph must have worked hard to provide food for Mary and Jesus. They both obeyed him because he was the head of the Holy Family. This was a very heavy responsibility for Joseph, and he prayed hard to God to make him a good

31

protector. God heard his prayers and even, when necessary, sent an angel to tell Joseph what he ought to do.

Now that he is in heaven St Joseph, who protected the Holy Family, protects the whole family of God, the Catholic Church. He is also the patron saint of fathers and of all workers.

There are other vocations for men, and one of the most important of these is the *priesthood*. This is a very beautiful vocation, because the priest administers the sacraments, and it is through the sacraments that we can live the divine life, the life of Jesus himself. A father gives his children all they need for their earthly lives, but a priest gives the life of heaven – the life of Jesus himself, the Son of God – to all the souls entrusted to him.

A priest is a father to all the souls God entrusts to his care, which is why we call him 'Father'. Even the head of the whole Church, the successor of St Peter, is called the 'Pope', a word which comes from the Latin for father.

The Church does not normally give permission for a married man to become a priest, and priests are not allowed to get married. This is so that priests can devote all their time and energy to looking after all the souls placed in their charge. If they were married they would have to concern themselves with the duties of a father's state of life. They would have to work and look after their wives and children, and so might not be able to look after souls so well.

The duties of a priest are to give himself completely to God and thus to men, and not to keep anything for himself. In particular he is expected to say Mass every day, and to administer the sacraments to the faithful. He also has to pray his *breviary*, a book which has all the psalms and prayers for each day. (Maybe you can ask a priest you know well to show you his breviary.) To do all this needs a lot of spiritual strength, and this strength God gives through his grace.

God's grace comes to the priest primarily from the Mass he celebrates each day, because the Mass is an inexhaustible source of all the graces, of all God's gifts. But every priest also needs our prayers. A priest with no one to pray for him is like a car without petrol, and a priest needs a family's prayers just as much as the family needs the priest.

The life of St John Vianney, the Curé d'Ars, provides a beautiful model for every priest. Do you know about him? He said to a young boy who told him the way to Ars, the village where he was to be the priest: 'You have shown me the way to Ars, now I will show you the way to Heaven'!

Don Bosco was an Italian priest and saint who did a lot for the education of youth. He has been made patron saint of many Catholic schools. Have you heard of him?

Questions

Do you know what St Joseph's job was? Why did he have to work?

What are the duties of a father? What are those of a priest?

What are the duties of your state of life?

Why are priests normally not married?

Does a priest have children?

How do we address priests? Why?

How does a priest enable us to share in the divine life?

Can you name and describe the seven sacraments? Which ones have you already received?

7

Original Sin, and why
God gave us Marriage

Do you know what *Original Sin* is?

No doubt you have heard about Adam and Eve, our first parents. Before Original Sin, Adam and Eve loved God, their Maker, with all their hearts. They lived with him in close friendship and obeyed him in everything. God had given them the gift of knowing and loving him: in other words, they had received from God the *supernatural life*, which is close friendship with God, who is the source of all that is right and good, and in particular the source of all love.

Adam and Eve, through being close to God, received from him a great capacity for love. They were able to love each other very deeply, without selfishness and without seeking their own satisfaction. Other than pleasing God, their only concern was to look after the happiness and well-being of each other.

But after Original Sin, what happened? Adam and Eve lost this great intimacy and close friendship with God. They disobeyed him because they didn't want to be obedient to him any longer. It was a sin of pride: they wanted to be like God, able to decide for themselves what was good and what was evil.

They stopped loving God and became afraid of him, and so they hid when they heard him in the garden. They lost their friendship with God, and no longer had the *supernatural life*. You can read the story of Original Sin in chapters two and three of Genesis, the first book of the Bible.

Because God is the source of all love, Adam and Eve no longer knew how to love each other properly. Selfishness entered their hearts and they put their own pleasure before the good of the other.

We are also affected by Original Sin, which is very serious and damaging for us. Adam and Eve couldn't pass on what they had lost, and so men and women no longer knew how to love properly!

Happily mankind was rescued from this condition when God gave us his Son to save us, and the sacraments through which we share his Son's life. By means of the sacraments we can not only recover the *supernatural life* which Adam and Eve enjoyed before Original Sin, but also share the very life of Jesus himself, becoming members of his mystical body. So the supernatural life which God offers us now is the *divine life* itself!

God, who loves children especially, knows that they need parents who love one another. So he has created a very special sacrament to give parents the strength to love each other deeply, to love each other *all their lives*, and to love each other with God's love. This sacrament is *the sacrament of marriage*.

God doesn't want Christians to live together like married couples without being united by this sacrament. He knows that without it, they could only draw upon their ordinary human strength to try to love each other and their children, just like Adam and Eve after Original Sin. Even if they were sincere and obtained a civil marriage at a Registry Office, they would be taking the risk, by depriving themselves of the power of the sacrament, of coming to grief and separating with a lot of damage to their hearts and souls. Their children would also suffer a great deal and would find themselves torn between their parents. Unhappily there are many children in this position nowadays, and we have to pray hard for them.

It is also for this reason that God doesn't want young men and women in love to do before they are married what is reserved for married couples. If they do this they risk completely spoiling their married life, especially the early moments of it, which should be among the most beautiful. Instead of receiving their partners from the hands of God, after their relationship has properly matured, they would be coming together without making a real choice – they would be building a house on sand and in haste, rather than patiently laying rock-solid foundations.

In the sacrament of marriage God gives a husband and wife, if they really want it, the power to love each other all through life without selfishness, the power to love all the children God gives them, and the power to bring them up and to build a Christian family. In other words, the sacrament of marriage is a fountain of the love of God from which the couple can continually draw the strength they need.

Of course it will be essential for the married couple to preserve the grace of their marriage by daily family prayer, by going as often as possible to Mass to receive the *Holy Eucharist* (Jesus himself *really present* in body and soul, in his human and divine natures, in the consecrated Host), and by receiving God's pardon regularly at *Confession* (the sacrament of Penance or Reconciliation).

These practices are essential if the husband and wife are to love each other all their lives with a love stronger than that of Adam and Eve before Original Sin – *the very love and the very life of Jesus*. But if they do pray and attend the sacraments they will be able to say with St Paul: *'It is no longer I who live, but Christ who lives in me'* (*Gal* 2: 20).

You must be surprised that we haven't mentioned Mary. It's time we did, as Original Sin is something she understood very well – precisely because she was free from it.

As a special privilege, so that she could be the mother of God the Son made Man, God gave Mary from the moment of her conception the grace of the divine life. He wanted Jesus to have a spotless cradle, totally unaffected by sin, and above all untouched by Original Sin.

This is why we call Mary *the Immaculate Conception*. Living so fully the divine life, she has her own special friendship with God, the source of all love. Because of this friendship she is able to love us much more than any mother or father ever could, and this is why Jesus gave her to us to be our Mother in Heaven.

We should always remember that she only gave us one command while on earth:

'Do whatever he tells you'.

Questions

Do you know what Original Sin is? What did Adam and Eve lose because of Original Sin?

How has God made it possible for us to recover the supernatural life?

Is the supernatural life he offers us now the same or better than the supernatural life of Adam and Eve? What did St Paul say on this subject?

What sacrament must a man and woman receive who want to have a family together? Why?

Is it right for a young woman and a young man who are in love to live together like husband and wife before they have received the sacrament of marriage? Why is it dangerous?

What must a couple do to keep the grace of the sacrament of marriage?

Why do we call Mary *the Immaculate Conception*?

What commandment did Our Lady give us during her earthly life?

Do you know about the apparitions of Our Lady at Fatima, at Guadaloupe, and at Lourdes? Do you know what she asked us to do at each of these apparitions?

8

Love is not so much
what you feel as what you do

This may seem surprising. You probably think that if you feel you love your parents, then you really love them. You perhaps imagine that when a young couple feel they love each other, they do in fact love each other.

Well, this is true in a certain sense of the word *love,* the sense that TV, newspapers or magazines use every day. But for Christians (and for well-instructed non-Christians, such as some of the ancient Greek philosophers), 'love' has a much stronger sense. To love someone doesn't mean, or doesn't only mean, to feel that you love them – it means constantly trying to *do* everything one can to help them and to make sure that everything goes well for them. The Greeks called this kind of love *agape*, which means a self-sacrificing love.

Parents love their children: they watch over them night and day. For the same reason they sometimes feel that they should correct their children. Because their love is not just a matter of *feeling*, but of *doing*, they feed them properly to make sure that they are healthy, and they get up in the night to comfort them when they are ill or frightened. They send them to school to learn things, so that they can find a job when they are grown up. They spend time with them, playing with them, and helping them to develop their minds and their characters. Sometimes this can be hard work for parents, but they do it out of love, because they want the best for their children.

41

In the same way, the husband and wife care for each other and support each other. Usually the husband has to go to work during the week, but he makes sure that he doesn't come home too late, so that he can help his wife. His wife takes care to keep the home clean and welcoming for her husband.

Because of their love they pay attention to each other in numerous small ways, they try not to upset each other, and they help each other in every way they can.

Sometimes these things can be difficult or tiring. The emotion of love can make matters a little easier – that is why God created it. But the emotion doesn't solve all problems, because it isn't always there. For example, after an argument (arguments happen from time to time because of our sinfulness) it is our decision to act lovingly which reconciles us and makes us forgive each other, not necessarily the loving feeling, which quite often disappears for a time.

Fortunately, a husband and wife who are regularly receiving the sacraments (Confession and especially Holy Communion) have an amazing asset, because they don't love one another with their own strength, but with the love Jesus has for his Church, and for all men. We know what Jesus was capable of in his love – he gave his life to save us from sin and death, and was even prepared to suffer death on a cross out of love for us. The love of Jesus for his Church is more than simply the model for love between a husband and wife. Through the sacraments, they can actually be filled with Jesus' love, so that they can say, with St Paul, 'It is no longer I who live, but Christ who lives in me' (*Gal* 2:20).

But to follow Jesus and to learn his way of loving, you have to learn to exercise your will-power, not just over other people, as anyone can, but over *yourself*. You have to learn to *serve* others.

If a mother and father are good parents, they do nothing

but serve: they are always at the service of their family and their children. Of course, their aim is not to give in to their children's whims, but to help them become good Christians who love God and their neighbour.

Priests, monks and nuns do exactly the same, giving up their lives to serve others.

From now on you should be preparing yourself to live in the service of others. It's really very easy. All you have to do is love and exercise your will-power (especially over yourself).

Here are some ideas:

– Help at home by laying or clearing the table, tidying up your clothes and toys, and doing your homework before going to play.

– Come straightaway when one of your parents calls and be ready to obey them with a smile (the smile is sometimes the difficult bit!)

– Switch off the TV as soon as your parents ask you to, or as soon as the programme you are watching starts to become offensive, violent or indecent (this can require a lot of will-power!).

– Stop spending time with bad friends who might lead you astray.

– Go to Mass cheerfully, because you love Jesus.

– Go regularly to communion and confession. *Nothing is more important than this*, because the sacraments make us grow in the love of God. The best idea is to go to confession once a month. Going frequently makes it less difficult.

– Be attentive and concentrate at family prayers each day.

If your parents forget to pray with you, remind them, because it is good for them as well as for you.

– Devote a little time each day to praying alone with God, with Jesus. Open your heart to him and listen to him.

You must have plenty of your own ideas too. Love is doing all of these things, because *loving means serving others*, following Jesus' loving example.

When you are older you will meet young men (if you are a girl) and young women (if you are a boy) and no doubt you will feel very fond of one or more of them.

This is when you have to be master of yourself, so that you can tell what your *vocation* is (what God wants you to do) without letting yourself be carried away by your feelings. You will need to be very careful about the strong emotions which we call *passions*. A *passion* is something that happens without our being able or wanting to resist it. To have true freedom we need to be able to choose what is good and right, to choose to do God's will, without being influenced or prevented by passion.

To learn about freedom is to learn about love and about serving others.

It is not easy, but when our own strength is not enough we have to ask God to give us his love, and then everything is possible.

Questions

Is love an emotion? What is it?

What do your parents do because they love you? What do you do because you love them? What do you do because you love Jesus and Mary?

44

What could you try to do better in order to love your parents more, and Jesus and Mary more? (Remember that Jesus must come first.)

Have you made your first communion? Do you go regularly to confession and communion? Why?

Do you pray in the morning and at night? Does your family pray together?

What did Mary say when the angel Gabriel asked her to be Jesus' mother? What do you say when God or your parents ask you to do something?

9

A girl's virginity

Boys should also read this!

When you give someone a present, it should be new, and given away for good. You don't give a present and say, 'Oh, well, I'll see, I might take it back one day if I feel like it!' What a poor present that would be, if you could take it back!

When a young woman gets married, she gives herself to her husband on their wedding day, giving herself to him as a wonderful present, a present from God. She should be pure, just as a present should be new, and she gives herself to him for good. (Of course it's exactly the same for her husband – he should be pure for his wife, and give himself to her for good – but here we are concerned with the young woman.)

So that they remember about this present for their husbands, God has marked girls with a physical sign, putting his seal on them. In the past when a nobleman wrote a letter, he had a way of making certain that no one except the person addressed would read it. The method he used was to fold the letter up and put a wax seal on it, marked with his own private sign. The person he had written to, the only person who had the right to read the letter, would then break the seal to open the letter.

God has done a very similar thing for girls. When she is pregnant, a woman shelters her children inside her until they are born, just as Jesus in the consecrated Host is sheltered in the tabernacle in church. So boys and fathers have to respect

47

young women and mothers because they are tabernacles of the mystery of life. The kind of tabernacle a girl has is closed by God's seal: a very fine, delicate *membrane* (sheet of skin) at the entrance to the vagina, called the *hymen.*

Once a young man and a young woman have got married, the husband can delicately open the entrance to this tabernacle by gently breaking the membrane in a beautiful action which expresses the couple's unity. This is the action by which they create new life: it is the secret of your parents' love.

God gives the husband the right to break the seal through the sacrament of Marriage. Without this sacrament, he does not have the right to do it, and the young woman does not have the right to let him do it.

The membrane, which is a seal from God, marks the *virginity* of every girl's body.

If a girl doesn't know she should keep her virginity and lets a boy do what should be saved for her husband, the membrane cannot be restored. She won't be able to give herself intact to her future husband on the day of their marriage.

Mary kept herself perfectly intact out of love for Jesus, and even Joseph didn't want to 'know' his wife, because he realised that Mary had consecrated herself entirely to God. (The word 'know' is the one used in Holy Scripture to describe the loving action by which a married couple create new life.) And so, even after she had become a mother, Mary kept her virginity, which is why we call her the *Blessed Virgin.*

Just as Mary kept her state of virginity in her body, she was also totally perfect in her soul. She never had an impure thought tempting her to seek sensual pleasure, nor displayed any mark of selfishness, nor ever lacked charity or respect for others.

In all these ways, every young woman should take Mary as her model. The virginity of the body is important, of course, but it is not as difficult to keep as the virginity of the soul. A daily struggle is needed for the soul to be kept pure.

You have to protect yourself from bad books, bad films, bad friends, and dubious behaviour. You have to close your eyes to indecent images, and close your ears and flee from dirty jokes, or cut them short because they have no good purpose. Such dirty talk merely cheapens what is beautiful, despoils what is pure, and profanes what is sacred. Sometimes you will have to listen to the silly comments of foolish people, who will always make more noise than those who think like you and want to protect their souls.

It will mean a struggle every day, but what a tremendous reward will be given to you in heaven, if you try to keep your soul pure like Mary's! What difficulties, what heartbreak you will be spared on earth! What a wonderful present you will have to give to your husband, if you get married, or to Jesus, if you become a nun! And finally you will be a powerful help to anyone you can comfort or support by your presence and your prayers, *because the purer you are, the more you are able to love*.

Is this purity impossibly difficult? Of course it is, if you rely only on your own strength – but not if you ask Mary fervently to help you, because she loves you with all her heart, and her Son can refuse her nothing.

Questions

What is the seal called which God gives every girl to mark her body's virginity? Where is it? What does it protect?

Why does God mark girls with his seal like this?

Can the membrane recover once it has been broken?

Can you explain these two titles of Mary: the *Immaculate Conception* and the *Blessed Virgin*? (Be careful not to confuse two very different things!)

There are two kinds of virginity. Can you name them?

What do you have to do to protect the virginity of your soul?

Do you want to keep your virginity? Both that of your body until you are married, and that of your soul all your life? Why?

Are you prepared to work hard at this? In what ways?

10

A boy's purity

Girls should also read this!

We have now talked about the virginity of girls – both the virginity of the body and that of the soul. How does this affect boys?

Of course boys are not tabernacles of the mystery of life. But even if this mystery isn't hidden within them, they are no less obliged to respect it, and to respect those in whom it is hidden.

And so a boy mustn't let himself play the same kind of games with girls, even his sisters, that he would with other boys. He must have even more respect for his mother, not only because she is a woman, but also because she is his mother, who has carried him since the first day of his existence, and watched over him and fed him.

This is why young men (or at least those worthy of the name) should let their mothers and other women go through doors in front of them, serve them first at table, and make sure that they pay them other small courtesies and attentions. All this is good, but there is still a long way to go.

A boy also has to keep his body and soul pure for his future wife, if he is going to marry, or for Christ, if he is called to be a priest or religious.

There are two reasons why it is harder for a boy than for a girl to keep himself pure.

Firstly, because some boys like to play at being tough and think it proves how clever they are if they say and do

crude things, or look at photographs and films in which women or men appear in vulgar poses or engage in impure activities.

This is animal behaviour, all the worse for the fact that not even animals do such things. People who do them are a danger to themselves, because they always destroy their souls, and sometimes destroy their bodies too. They are a danger to others, because their example attracts boys of weak character and leads them into impurity too.

The second reason why it is hard for boys to keep themselves pure is that they are aware, in a different way from girls, of the changes in their bodies and new bodily functions which come with *puberty* – the age at which a boy becomes a young man and has the capacity to become a father.

A girl regularly has her periods, which remind her that God offers her the opportunity to be the source of new life. A boy notices, among other things, changes in his *genitals*, the organs which enable him to be the source of new life. From time to time his penis fills out and becomes hard – we say he has an *erection* – and this is what allows him to become a father. When he has an erection, he can delicately use his penis to put millions of his sperm into the vagina of his wife, in the beautiful act of love which God reserves for married couples. An erection is caused by blood filling the spongy tissue which the penis is made of. However it doesn't always happen at a convenient time, and can sometimes happen for no reason at all.

This bodily function can be the occasion of sin against purity, if, incited by bad reading, bad films or bad company, a boy lets himself play with his body.

This kind of playing is a silly and purely selfish pastime. Like the lie the serpent told to Eve, it can give the impression that it is simply a means to pleasurable sensations, when in fact it brings with it bitterness and disgust and can destroy the soul.

It is even more dangerous because if it is repeated, very bad habits can be set up, habits which rapidly turn into a kind of slavery. Disguised as a friend, evil enters the soul and masters it, making it as hard as stone.

And so boys must keep clear of this kind of behaviour and of anything which might lead them to it. God entrusted us with our bodies for doing good, not evil, and we will all have to account to God for what we have done with them. St Paul said 'Your body is a temple of the Holy Spirit within you, which you have from God. You are not your own; you were bought with a price. So glorify God in your body' (*I Cor* 6: 19-20).

If you are tempted, avoid being alone, and seek out the company of your parents, brothers or sisters, or the kind of friends who will influence you to the good, not to the bad. If when you are older you need to burn up energy, go out and run a mile – or two miles, if one is not enough!

If there is nobody around to provide you with company, there is always the fellowship of heaven.

– Pray to Mary, throwing yourself into her arms.

– Your guardian angel is waiting for you to ask his help.

– St Michael the Archangel is also on the watch – he chased Lucifer from heaven, and will chase him from your soul.

– Maybe you have grandparents or other relatives, or even a little brother or sister who care for you from heaven.

– If recourse to this help is not enough, remember that God is the witness of all your thoughts.

Girls: you must help boys by suitable behaviour, and by a modesty of appearance reflecting your purity of soul. You must also pray for the boy whom you don't yet know but who, if it is God's will, will one day be your husband. At this very moment he is fighting the battle of purity, like all boys, and he already needs your help!

Questions

How should boys be polite towards young women and mothers? Why do they have to be polite?

Do you steer clear of coarse boys who get pleasure from crude stories?

Does your body belong to you? Who gave it to you? Can you do whatever you like with it? Why not?

Who is St Michael? What did he do? What can he do for each one of us?

Do you remember to ask your Guardian Angel to watch over you?

Prayer to your Guardian Angel

Angel of God, my guardian dear,
to whom God's love commits me here,
ever this day be at my side,
to light and guard, to rule and guide.
Amen.

Prayer to St Michael

Holy Michael Archangel, defend us in the day
of battle, be our safeguard against the wicked-
ness and snares of the devil. May God rebuke
him we humbly pray, and do thou, prince of
the heavenly host, by the power of God thrust
down to hell Satan and all wicked spirits who
wander through the world for the ruin of
souls. *Amen.*

The prodigal son (*Luke* 15:11-32)

11

Temptations, falls, forgiveness

As you know, there are unfortunately many different ways to fall into sin. We are tempted to be greedy, to be insolent, lazy, violent; to be dishonest or to lie; to be impure, selfish and proud. The television can be one major way the devil encourages us to do wrong.

It is important for you to know that on your own, with your own strength, you will not be able to resist temptation. If you think that on your own you are always strong enough to resist the devil, you have already committed a serious sin of pride, because no one can resist his assault just with their own strength. The whole company of heaven is ready to come to your aid, just as soon as you ask!

You also know that if you fall, you have nothing to worry about so long as you go as quickly as possible to ask Jesus for his forgiveness, with sincere regret and with a firm resolution to do everything possible to avoid sinning again.

Go to confession regularly, because if you are used to refreshing your soul every so often, then you will live a better life day by day, and if an 'accident' happens, you'll find it easy to throw yourself into God's arms once more. There are also ways of making confession easier:

– Make an examination of conscience as often as you can (every day is best). All we have to do is take the commandments of God and the commandments of the Church one by one and ask ourselves seriously and honestly how well we have followed them. If you have forgotten any of them, relearn them, and if necessary, write an examination of conscience on a piece of card for yourself.

– It is good to prepare your confession beforehand, by writing down what you have to say on a piece of paper. There is nothing shameful about having to do this. If you do it you will avoid saying the first thing that comes into your head because you can't remember your sins once you are in the confessional. This isn't something just for children – many adults do it and find it very helpful.

– Say whatever you find most difficult first, even if it doesn't seem to be the most serious sin. Once you have said it, the rest will be easy.

– While you are preparing your confession, as well as examining your conscience, you should try to see if you have made any progress or special efforts since your last confession. The best way of fighting our most persistent faults is to develop our strongest virtues at the same time, so that these have a good influence on the rest of our souls.

Afterwards, don't forget to make a note of your resolutions for the future.

Above all, you mustn't get discouraged if, despite firm resolutions, you still fall again and again into the same faults – rather you should be patient and persevere. The most serious sin after indifference (not caring) is despair of Jesus' mercy. Even when you are fed up with saying sorry, he is never fed up with pardoning you.

Do you know what the difference was between St Peter and Judas? They both betrayed Our Lord – one of them denied him three times, and the other gave him up to be crucified. But St Peter wept at his fault and asked Jesus' pardon, whereas Judas thought that he would never be pardoned – and hanged himself!

St Peter's sin was certainly very serious, so serious that to remind us of his sin, and Jesus' pardon, clocktowers on churches often have a cockerel on top, because the cock crowed three times after St Peter betrayed Jesus.

Perhaps one day you will be close to someone who has behaved badly and regrets it. Help him, telling him that Jesus will forgive him, and will give him peace in his soul, which will become as white as snow. Of course, for serious sins, there is always regret, pain to live with, a scar in the heart, and sometimes in the body, but this pain is much lighter when one knows one is forgiven by God.

It is God, and only God, who can really repair the wrongs which we have done to others and to ourselves. He does it in his own way, which is rarely ours, but he always does it. And the pain and regret which remain we can offer to Jesus, so that he can add them to his Cross, to save other souls who are committing the same sins, and who haven't yet taken themselves to him to ask his forgiveness.

Questions

Have you made your first communion? Have you been to confession since? Do you go regularly? If not, why don't you make a resolution to go more often (monthly is ideal)?

Should we go back to confession even if, despite our resolutions, we commit the same sins again?

What is the opposite of despair? Do you know the Act of Hope? If not ask your parents or a priest to teach you it.

When we have sinned and been to confession what happens to our soul? Does something remain after serious sins? What can we do about it?

12

What is freedom?

You are bound to come across people who will encourage you to do what is wrong, and they are very likely to try to make things that are wrong look attractive. Often they will make fun of you, or even threaten you if you won't go along with them. But evil is always the same – it comes to you as a friend, but becomes a tyrant inside you if you let it in!

Some people may offer you drugs. These are dangerous chemicals which can be smoked (hash, marijuana), inhaled as liquids (glue, ether) or powders (cocaine), stuck onto your skin (plasters which release the drug through the skin into your blood), or injected with a syringe.

You must always refuse these drugs because they very quickly take control of you, rather than you controlling them. Day by day you would come to need a stronger dose or even a harder drug, and this process almost always ends with madness and finally death.

You must be careful too because you can often be offered drugs in a form which looks entirely innocent, such as a cigarette.

Tobacco itself, in its ordinary form, can also enslave you. Smoking is always harmful, and if you start before you are 18 or 20 the problem is even worse because it can check your growth, and may one day lead to lung or other cancers. If you want to try smoking, you should do it only in front of your parents and with their permission. Refuse any cigarettes your friends offer you, and if they consider you foolish, too bad. Let them say what they want, you can be sure that you are right. Smokers tend to lose their free will (and their freedom), as they find it very hard to do without tobacco.

You will doubtless also be offered alcohol, and again, you must adamantly refuse, and only drink wine, beer or spirits when you are in your parents' company, with their permission. Alcohol abuse leads to people losing control of their lives in just the same way as drug-taking. It kills more slowly, but just as surely. When we are under the influence of alcohol we are often led to do the most stupid and abominable things.

Finally, you will certainly see girls and boys kissing and cuddling, making indecent suggestions, and trying to get you to do the same, or even boasting of doing what should be reserved for their future husbands or wives.

All these people will tell you that freedom is doing whatever you want to do, whatever suggests itself to you, but how wrong they are! That kind of freedom is merely the freedom of an animal which is controlled by desires, sensations and passions. A person who pursues this kind of freedom is as free as a boat without a rudder, a sail or a motor, lost at sea, at the mercy of the wind, the currents, the reefs. Such a person is sure to be shipwrecked!

True freedom has nothing to do with being enslaved by these bad habits, which are very often deadly for the soul, and sometimes deadly for the body too. *True liberty means being able to do freely what is good and pleasing to God.*

When monks and nuns make a vow of poverty (which means they commit themselves to having no possessions), they do so in order to be free. Freedom means not being attached to anything which could prevent their souls from becoming united with God.

For parents it is more difficult, because their state of life obliges them to have a home for their family to live in and a job to ensure they can feed and clothe their children. They also need a degree of comfort and financial security to help them bring up their children. It is very difficult for parents to stay free in their hearts and not to become attached to these things more than is necessary. That is why one priest has said that *'a religious vocation is the highway to sanctity'*. The vocation of parents is by contrast longer, like a country road. But the destination is the same – *we are all called to become saints!*

What about you? You have reached the age of reason, the age when you start to become responsible for your life, your free will, your body, and your soul. *Do you want to stay free*, to be able to follow the call God will make known to you when the time is right, or do you prefer to give up your free will and allow yourself to be enslaved by all the bad things that will come your way? Your parents are there to help you, but they can't always be just behind you (which you wouldn't like anyway), so *it's up to you to choose*.

If you make the right choice you can go straight to work by exercising your free will over yourself. It won't be too difficult, because *love is the best exercise of the will* – loving God, your parents, everyone around you. Only be sure that your love is not an emotion, or at least not just an emotion. *You also need actions*, and it is not always the visible ones which have the greatest value.

Questions

What are the most important things to stay away from if you want to be free?

What is the age of reason? What is real freedom?

Why is a religious vocation the highway to sanctity?

What is the best way of exercising your free will?

The rich young man
Matthew 19:16-30, *Mark* 10:17-31, *Luke* 18:18-39

13

Making a commitment

You have now read through this book, and we hope that it has enlightened you and will help you. We have written it with love.

Perhaps you would like to know that we are Christian parents, to whom God has given four children (so far). We hope that in a few years, our sons and daughters will be honest, upright and free with the true freedom of children of God. We hope this will be true for you too, even though we don't know you.

Do you want to give yourself a goal for the years to come? Do you want to keep your freedom, so that one day you can without difficulty respond to God's vocation for you? Are you prepared to make an effort to do this, and to commit yourself to making this effort?

If your answer is yes, we suggest that you make a special declaration, one which is designed to help you, not to hinder you. This declaration is easy, and its burden light. It is designed to be suitable for you. If you were to break it, by breaking one of the commandments of God or of the Church, you would not have done any extra wrong by breaking the declaration.

We think that this commitment can really help you in the years to come, years which will be decisive for the rest of your life.

If you wish to make this commitment, you simply have to copy the appropriate text (for a girl or boy) onto a piece of paper, and date and sign it. You can give it to a grown-up you particularly trust, or, better still, to a priest you know well, asking them to pray regularly for you, and to remind you of it from time to time. (You should pray regularly for them in return.) Or you can just keep the paper with your own things, without telling anyone, making it a secret between you and God, and reminding yourself of it from time to time by re-reading the paper.

You should feel free to do this only if it is what you want, not if you are doing it to please anyone other than God. But if you make the declaration you can be sure that your reward will be much greater than the effort made to live up to it.

For a girl

I the undersigned ...., a Christian girl, wish to keep my freedom as a child of God so that I am able, when the time comes, to answer God's call either to enter the religious life or a life of consecrated celibacy, or to become a Christian wife and mother, whichever he wishes.

To this end, before Jesus and Mary his most holy Mother, I commit myself for my whole life to following the commandments of God and the Catholic Church, and in particular I undertake:

– to pray each morning and evening, and also to spend some moments during the day privately with God;

– never to miss Mass on Sundays or holydays of obligation;

– to go to confession regularly, at least before important feasts (Christmas, Easter, the Assumption and All Saints);

– to keep my virginity until marriage, if that is my vocation, otherwise all my life;

– to keep my soul pure by prudent behaviour, firmly avoiding anything contrary to chastity.

I ask Mary, my mother in Heaven, for her intercession that I may obtain the graces necessary for keeping this commitment as faithfully as possible.

In the event that I break this commitment in any way, I ask Jesus, my Saviour, in advance for his mercy and for the courage to return as soon as possible to the commitments I have made.

I offer him in advance the efforts which I will make and the sufferings I may undergo in keeping this commitment, for the sake of the Holy Souls and for ....
(write here the intention of your choice)

I ask my Guardian Angel and St Michael for their constant assistance in keeping this resolution.

    Signed...

    at ....

    the .... day of ....

For a boy

I the undersigned ...., a Christian boy, wish to keep my freedom as a child of God so that I am able, when the time comes, to answer God's call to become a priest, to lead the religious life, or to become a Christian husband and father, whichever he wishes.

To this end, before Jesus and Mary his most Holy Mother, I commit myself for my whole life to following the commandments of God and the Catholic Church, and in particular I undertake:

- to pray each morning and evening, and to spend some moments during the day privately with God;

- never to miss Mass on Sundays or holydays of obligation;

- to go to confession regularly, at least before important feasts (Christmas, Easter, the Assumption and All Saints);

- to practise purity of body and soul, both in my actions and in my thoughts, through prudent behaviour, firmly avoiding anything contrary to chastity, and in particular keeping myself pure for my wife (if marriage is my vocation).

I ask Mary, my mother in Heaven, to intercede for me that I may obtain the graces necessary for keeping this commitment as faithfully as possible.

In the event that I break this commitment in any way, I ask Jesus my Saviour for his mercy and for the courage to return as soon as possible to the commitments I have made.

I offer him in advance the efforts I will make and the sufferings I may undergo in keeping this commitment, for the sake of the Holy Souls and for ....
(write here the intention of your choice)

    I ask my Guardian Angel and St Michael for their constant assistance in keeping this resolution.

    Signed..

    at...

    the ....day of ....

Conclusion

So now you have committed yourself to a careful following of the commandments. This is good, but not something to boast about, for it is the minimum required of a Christian.

When Jesus was on earth there was a rich young man who was good and kind and had 'done the minimum' since childhood. Let's hear what St Mark wrote about him in chapter 10 of his Gospel.

> As he was setting out on his journey, a man ran up and knelt before him, and asked him, 'Good teacher, what must I do to inherit eternal life?' And Jesus said to him, 'Why do you call me good? No one is good but God alone. You know the commandments: Do not kill, Do not commit adultery, Do not steal, Do not bear false witness, Do not defraud, Honour your father and mother'. And he said to him, 'Teacher, all these I have observed from my youth'. And Jesus looking upon him loved him, and said to him, 'You lack one thing; go, sell what you have, and give to the poor, and you will have treasure in heaven; and come, follow me.' At that saying his countenance fell, and he went away sorrowful; for he had great possessions.

There are many things we can take from this text, so many that Pope John Paul II has written an *encyclical* about them, a letter to all Christians, called *The Splendour of Truth*.

All we can do is concentrate on a few phrases relevant to our present concerns.

73

No-one is good but God alone. That's right: it's not up to us or to you to decide what is good and what is bad – we cannot make up our own morality. Neither the TV nor your friends can tell you what is right or wrong. Only the Church can teach you morality, through the commandments, the gospels, the epistles, and the words of the Holy Father. The Holy Father never stops encouraging young people to practise chastity and purity, which alone can make them happy.

Jesus, looking at him, loved him. Respect for the commandments of God and the Church really is important. Such respect guarantees that Jesus will have a special affection for us, just as he did for the rich young man. We know, from what Jesus himself said, that if we are baptised, if we follow the commandments, if we receive the sacraments regularly, we will have God's grace and eternal life. The same message is clear from the Act of Hope: 'My God, I hope with a firm confidence, that you will give me your grace in this world, and if I respect your commandments, eternal happiness in the world to come, because you have promised us this and you always keep your promises'.

Come, . . . follow me. The path to sanctity means following Jesus – even to the foot of the Cross. To be sure, he doesn't ask for the kind of acts of heroism that we dream about. Rather, Jesus asks us each day to follow him, to be faithful to him and to offer to him, in order to please him, the little crosses – even the smallest crosses – made up of all our little sacrifices, our good deeds which we do with a smile for love of him. This is what following Jesus, and saving souls with him, really means. St Paul said:

'It is no longer I who live, but Christ who lives in me'.

Of course you could reply that Jesus has never spoken to you like this, or that you are not the rich young man. How can you be so sure? Do what the young man did, going down on your knees before Jesus and asking him what you must do to save souls and win eternal life. Contemplate Jesus, your Lord, suffering on the Cross, adore him, and really open your eyes and heart to him.

May Mary guide and protect you, and may your guardian angel watch over you.

Catherine and Bernard